Contents

Key stories: 'One Snowy Night'

From 'One Snowy Night' by Nick Butterworth

It's cold in the park in winter. But Percy the park keeper doesn't mind.

He puts on his warm coat and his big scarf and wears two pairs of woolly socks inside his wellington boots.

Percy likes to be out in the fresh air.

In the middle of the park there is a little hut. This is where Percy lives.

When it gets too cold to be outside, Percy goes into his hut where it's cosy and warm.

Get started

Find the sentences in the story and write the missing words.

1. It's cold in the park in _winter_.

2. But _____ the park keeper doesn't mind.

3. Percy likes to be out in the _____ air.

4. In the _____ of the park there is a little hut.

Try these

Answer these questions. Use the story to help you.

1. What is Percy's job?

2. Where does Percy live?

3. What has Percy got on his feet?

4. What is it like in the hut?

Now try these

1. What do you think the park is like in summer?

2. Draw a picture of Percy in his hut.

3. Draw and label all the things Percy puts on to keep warm. With a partner, add other things he could wear.

Fairy stories: 'Hansel and Gretel'

From 'Hansel and Gretel' by Malachy Doyle

"There is no food," said the woodman.

"How will we eat?"

"Take Hansel and Gretel for a walk in the Brown Wood," said his wife, "and leave them."

"No!" said the woodman. "I cannot!"

"You must, or we will all die!" cried his wife.

So the woodman took Hansel and Gretel into the Brown Wood.

He gave the boy and girl some cake to eat.

But Hansel put it in his pocket and dropped little bits all along the way.

Get started

Find the sentences in the story and write the missing words.

1. "There is no _____," said the woodman.

2. "How will we _____?"

3. So the woodman took Hansel and _____ into the Brown Wood.

4. He gave the boy and girl some _____ to eat.

Try these

Answer these questions. Use the story to help you.

1. Who is in the story?

2. What is the problem?

3. Where did the woodman take the children?

4. What did he give them?

Now try these

1. Why do you think Hansel dropped bits of cake?

2. Draw a picture of Hansel dropping bits of cake.

3. Draw and label Hansel and Gretel when they are left in the woods. With a partner, plan what they can do next. Add a sentence to your picture to explain what their plan is.

Traditional tales: 'The King of the Forest'

From 'The King of the Forest' by Saviour Pirotta

A fox was having a nap. Suddenly a tiger leapt out at him.

"I've got you!"

The fox trembled. How could he save himself?

But then the fox had an idea. He said to the tiger, "How dare you touch the king of the forest?"

The tiger said, "The lion is the king of the forest."

The fox replied, "Everyone bows down before me now. Let go of me, and I'll show you."

Get started

Find the sentences in the tale and write the missing words.

1. A _____ was having a nap.

2. Suddenly a tiger _____ out at him.

3. But then the fox had an _____.

4. Everyone _____ down before me now.

Try these

Answer these questions. Use the tale to help you.

1. What was the fox doing before the tiger leapt out?

2. What did the fox do when the tiger leapt out?

3. Who did the fox say he was?

4. Who did the tiger think was king of the forest?

Now try these

1. Do you think the fox's plan is clever? Why?

2. Draw a picture of the fox having a nap.

3. Draw a picture of the fox and the tiger in the forest. With a partner, think of what they will say next. Add speech bubbles to show what they will say.

Rhymes and poems: 'Cats'

Cats sleep
Anywhere,
Any table,
Any chair,
Top of piano,
Window-ledge,
In the middle,
On the edge,
Open drawer,
Empty shoe,
Anybody's
Lap will do
Fitted in a cardboard box
In the cupboard
With your frocks –
Anywhere!
They don't care!
Cats sleep
Anywhere.

Eleanor Farjeon

Get started

Find the lines in the poem and write the missing words.

1. Cats sleep _____

2. Any table, Any _____

3. Anybody's _____ will do

4. Fitted in a _____ box

Try these

Answer these questions. Use the poem to help you.

1. What is in the cupboard with the cat?

2. Where on the window-ledge will cats sleep?

3. Where do cats sleep? List three places.

4. What word in the poem sounds like 'ledge'?

Now try these

1. Why do you think cats will sleep anywhere?

2. Draw a picture of a cat sleeping in a shoe.

3. As a class, say the poem aloud. Repeat the poem and try to remember the words when your teacher pauses.

   Then write down the pairs of words that sound the same. Read the pairs of words aloud to a partner. With your partner, add other words that sound like them.

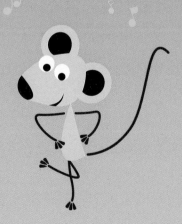

Rhymes and poems: 'Honey Bear'

There was a big bear
Who lived in a cave;
His greatest love
Was honey.
He had two pence a week
Which he never could save,
So he never had
Any money.
I bought him a money box
Red and round,
In which to put
His money.
He saved and saved
Till he got a pound,
Then he spent it all
On honey.

Elizabeth Lang

Get started

Find the lines in the poem and write the missing words.

1. There was a big _____ Who lived in a cave

2. His greatest _____ was honey

3. I bought him a _____ box

4. He _____ and saved

Try these

Answer these questions. Use the poem to help you.

1. What did the bear love most?

2. How much money did the bear get each week?

3. What did the money box look like?

4. What word in the poem sounds like 'round'?

Now try these

1. Why do you think the bear could never save?

2. Draw a picture of the bear eating honey.

3. As a class, say the poem aloud. Repeat the poem and try to remember the words when your teacher pauses.

With a partner, list things that make you want to spend your money. Draw a poster to remind you and the bear to 'Save, Don't Spend!'

Rhymes and poems: 'A Chubby Little Snowman'

A chubby little snowman
Had a carrot nose;
Along came a rabbit
And what do you
suppose?
That hungry little bunny,
Looking for his lunch,
 ATE the snowman's carrot
nose ...
Nibble, nibble, CRUNCH!

Anon

Get started

Find the lines in the poem and write the missing words.

1. A chubby little _____

2. Had a _____ nose

3. That _____ little bunny

4. ATE the snowman's carrot

_____

Try these

Answer these questions. Use the poem to help you.

1. Who had a carrot nose?

2. Who was hungry?

3. What did the bunny do to the snowman?

4. What does 'chubby' mean? Ask a teacher for help if you need to.

Now try these

1. How did the bunny feel before he ate the carrot nose? How do you think he felt after he ate it?

2. Draw and label a picture of the snowman before the bunny comes.

3. As a class, say the poem aloud. Repeat the poem and try to remember the words when your teacher pauses.

Draw a picture of the snowman after the bunny has taken his carrot nose. With a partner, think about what happens next. Add a sentence to your picture to explain what happens next.

Reading instructions: Test your taste buds

You will need: grated apple, grated pear and grated carrot in three separate bowls; a spoon; a blindfold.

1. Put on the blindfold and hold your nose.

2. Ask a friend to feed you a spoonful from each of the three bowls. Can you tell which food is which?

3. Try the same thing again without holding your nose. This time, it should be much easier to tell the foods apart.

Get started

Find the sentences in the instructions and write the missing words.

1. Put on the _____ and hold your nose.

2. Ask a friend to feed you a _____ from each of the three bowls.

3. Can you tell which _____ is which?

4. Try the same thing again without _____ your nose.

Try these

Answer these questions. Use the instructions to help you.

1. What do you need for this test?

2. How many instructions are there?

3. What should you do before your friend feeds you?

4. How do you know in what order to do the instructions?

Now try these

1. Draw and label a picture of two friends doing this test.

2. With a partner, do this test. Write a sentence about what you found out.

Reading recounts: 'Man on the Moon'

From 'Man on the Moon' by Simon Bartram

This is where Bob lives. Every morning he rises at six o'clock. He has a cup of tea and two eggs for breakfast, before leaving for the rocket launch-pad. On the way he stops to buy a newspaper and some chocolate toffees.

He's on his way to work ...

... on the MOON!

Get started

Find the sentences in the recount and write the missing words.

1. Every _____ he rises at six o'clock.

2. He has a cup of tea and two eggs for _____, before leaving for the rocket launch-pad.

3. On the way he stops to _____ a newspaper and some chocolate toffees.

4. He's on his way to _____ ... ... on the MOON!

Try these

Answer these questions. Use the recount to help you.

1. What does Bob do first in the morning?

2. What does Bob get to read on the way to work?

3. What sweets does Bob like?

4. Where does Bob work?

Now try these

1. How do you think Bob feels about his job?

2. Draw a picture of Bob eating breakfast.

3. Draw a picture of yourself eating breakfast. What are you eating? Add a sentence to your picture to explain what you are eating. With a partner, talk about what else you do in the morning. Add one more sentence to your picture to explain what else you do in the morning.

Reading reports: 'Your Nose'

From 'Your Nose' by Nick Arnold and Maurizio De Angelis

A nose can be big. A nose can be small. Your nose is hard on top and soft at the end. It hurts when you bang your nose. Your nose has two nostrils. There are hairs in the nostrils and they are wet inside. You have snot in your nose.

Get started

Find the sentences in the report and write the missing words.

1. A _____ can be big.

2. Your nose is hard on _____ and soft at the end.

3. It _____ when you bang your nose.

4. Your nose has two _____.

Try these

Answer these questions. Use the report to help you.

1. Where on the body is your nose?

2. What size can a nose be?

3. Which part of the nose is soft?

4. What do nostrils have inside?

Now try these

1. Why do you think you have a nose?

2. Draw and label a picture of a nose.

3. Look at your eye in a mirror. Draw and label a picture of an eye. With a partner, think of two facts about eyes and add them to your picture.